HOW TO OBTAIN FAVOR WITH YOUR KING

MILLIE JACKSON

authorHOUSE®

AuthorHouse™
1663 Liberty Drive
Bloomington, IN 47403
www.authorhouse.com
Phone: 833-262-8899

Published by AuthorHouse 04/10/2023

ISBN: 979-8-8230-0576-0 (sc)
ISBN: 979-8-8230-0577-7 (e)

Library of Congress Control Number: 2023906460

Print information available on the last page.

This book is printed on acid-free paper.

God gave women intuition and femininity.
Used properly, the combination easily jumbles
the brain of any man I've ever met.
—Farrah Fawcett

You are a queen. Of all the women in the world, you were chosen by your king to reign with him. You are his queen. You are not his chambermaid, one whose only duty is to sweep, mop, dust, wash dishes and clothes, and cook his meals. No, your role as queen involves so much more than that. You are not a concubine or woman of low status. You are not a slave whose duty it is to be impregnated and bear his children, who will never be considered as worthy to become his wife—his queen. You are a queen, not one who cohabitates or shacks up with someone else's king. No, you are not a side piece; you are a queen, and *queens rule*.

As copastor of my church, I have had many opportunities to minister to women in their pursuit to have a successful marriage relationship. The biggest hindrance I have noticed is in the ability of these women to convey the truest feelings and deepest emotions to their spouses. Some women in their effort to be truthful and transparent tend to blurt out exactly how they feel without applying good communication skills. In essence, the issue, it seems, is not what to say, but how to say it. Although this book is written to help women effectively communicate with their spouses, the information presented is useful for communicating with anyone. Good communication is vital to the success of any solid relationship.

> Let your speech be always *with grace, seasoned with salt*, that ye may know how ye ought to answer every man. (Colossians 4:6 KJV)

It is possible to be very candid about your feelings in a way that does not alienate your spouse but will leave his manhood intact and achieve the desired results. It's all in how you say it. This book will teach how to say what you need to say and how to obtain the results you want. But let us first identify a few communication killers.

Never Say Never

Please ladies, *never say_never.* When you say to your spouse, "You *never* do this or that," even if he has only done it once, you just cut off the lines of communication. The only word your spouse heard you say was *never.* And never isn't true, even if he only did it once. If he continues to talk to you, it will be only to plead his case that never is just not true.

Another communication killer is "always" or "every time." A more truthful communication might include words like, "rarely, usually, or hardly ever." When communicating with your spouse, you must be very specific. Don't embellish because it makes you feel good for the moment. You will lose in the end.

Men are attracted to women because of their beauty, loveliness, style, polish, and charm. These are all synonyms of *grace;* therefore it is grace that will capture his attention. So whenever women come across as tough, harsh, callous, or grumpy, we lose their interest. Because he is a man, he is going to take a stance, and most likely he is not going to budge.

So when you speak, pay close attention to your tone, temperament, and timing. You're a woman. Use what you have; make your voice lovely, soft, and sweet.

> A *soft answer* turneth away wrath: but grievous words stir up anger. (Proverbs 15:1 ESV)

Rather than turn away, your spouse will turn to you and give ear to what you have to say. He will be less likely to become angry and more likely to consider what you ask. This is where patience comes into action. You noticed that I said, "*More* likely to consider what you ask." Many women have an issue in this area and want an immediate response. An immediate response oftentimes isn't the response hoped for.

Men need to feel in control of their domain. They have a king mentality and appreciate the submissiveness of their women and children; so when you have allowed him time to deliberate, you will get a more favorable response. Wait for it! Don't pressure him; remain patient and give him time to reflect on your kindly spoken words. It shows you trust his timing and decision-making process, and most likely things will work out in your favor.

> Likewise, ye wives, be in subjection to your own husbands; that, if any obey not the word, they also may without the word be won by the conversation of the

> wives; While they behold your chaste
> conversation coupled with fear. (1 Peter
> 3:1–2 KJV)

We are not talking about being manipulative. A man can see through that a mile away. But we're talking about the chaste conversation, which is so attractive to God and to men. A chaste conversation is having a pure lifestyle and no ulterior motives. Rather, that the thing you desire is best for the both of you not only for yourself. Ultimately, you want your spouse to begin to trust you and know that you are also looking out for his best interest.

> The heart of her husband doth safely
> trust in her … She will do him good and
> not evil all the days of her life. (Proverbs
> 31:11a–12 KJV)

Once this type of trustful atmosphere is established, you're on your way to becoming an honored and cherished partner in the relationship. There's not much your spouse wouldn't be willing to do for you.

For many years, I will admit, I had a very fuzzy concept of submission or subjection to my husband. I had always been an independent woman, and I had done an OK job of handling my business. Submission sounded to me like a dirty word. I felt as if I was being controlled. And I didn't like it. Because I didn't like it, I had a bucking type of spirit. I see that spirit in some women today. They buck against whatever the husbands have to say as if they must be in control. They view submission as weakness rather than meekness, which is power under control.

God gave me this analogy one day. I thought of a stallion, a big powerful creature with the ability to throw his rider at will. The rider may think he must break the stallion in order to ride him, but in reality he begins to build a relationship with him. The truth of the matter is that when he mounts the horse and is not thrown, it isn't because the stallion no longer has the ability to throw the rider. He can throw the rider at any time. He still has the power and capacity to do so, but because of their relationship, the stallion chooses to let the rider mount him and ride. Woman, you are not weak when you are submissive to your husband. You still have the power and the ability to wreak havoc if you so desire. But because you are wise, and you want to keep the relationship intact, you choose to submit.

> Every *wise woman* buildeth her house:
> but the foolish plucketh it down with
> her hands. (Proverbs 14:1 KJV)

No one can break you. No one can force you to do anything. You are not defeated. You are still powerful, full of strength and wisdom. You have a strategic plan. You know exactly what you are doing, why you are doing it, and your motives are pure. You are the architect of your home.

Timing, Text, Tone, and Temperament

Timing, text, tone, and temperament are important components in effectively communicating with your spouse. The words used in communication can connect or disconnect the listener. The key is to be precise when expressing your feelings. But first you must get in touch with yourself and your emotions. It is important to familiarize yourself with a list of possible emotions. Though the ranges of emotions are seemingly endless, knowledge of them will give you opportunity to accurately describe your feelings to your spouse. For example, you might say that you were hurt by a particular incident, but actually you felt irritated and aggravated by it instead. Whereas, hurt would mean damaged or wounded; what you actually meant is that you were annoyed or rubbed the wrong way. In this case, choosing the right adjective helps to accurately convey how you feel.

It eliminates wasted time explaining to your spouse how you could be hurt by something he considers trivial. It allows you to address why the behavior annoys you. (List provided in notes at the back of the book.)

"You" Statements

Let's talk about "you" statements. Those are the ones that start out putting the emphasis on the listener, who usually will decode the message that he is to blame. "You" statements generally come off sounding like accusations and will not usually elicit a positive response. "You" statements will send your spouse into combat mode, and he will defend himself. Oftentimes, the defensive stance will obstruct the conversation from moving forward. You could be stuck there for hours or days without ever touching on the real issue, which is whatever information that would have come after "you."

This is where getting in touch with your feelings will be advantageous. This is when you look at your feelings list of adjectives and find the word(s) that best describe how you feel and say, "because of that statement/what happened/how that situation played out, I feel this way or that way." You are only conveying *your* feelings; you aren't blaming anyone for the way you feel but simply providing insight. This type of communication eliminates unnecessary talk. It allows you to move right to the issue. You have also accepted full responsibility for your feelings as well as your responses. It is very liberating to hold the reins of your emotions rather than to put them in the hands of someone else. That, my dear, is true power.

Body Language

When about to approach a serious issue with your spouse, your body language and even your appearance can speak volumes. There is what is known as the 7 percent rule where communication is concerned. A study by Albert Mehrabian in his book *Silent Messages* assigned 7 percent to actual words, 38 percent to tone and music of the voice, and 55 percent to the weight of the speaker's body language. Another study concluded that body language is a more accurate indicator of meaning and emotions than actual words.

Your facial expression may be the most revealing of all. Your eyes will reveal emotions that words cannot express. People make statements like, "I didn't say a word; I just looked at him," not realizing that they have said more than a mouthful.

When we look into the eyes of a person, we often can discern the intentions of that person's heart. The eyes will tell if the person is interested or bored, angry or pleased. Your eyes radiate what is in your soul. Whether it is good or evil, your eyes will tell the story.

> The only source of light for the body is the eye. If you look at people and want to help them, you will be full of light. But if you look at people in a selfish way, you will be full of darkness. And if the only light you have is really darkness, you have the worst kind of darkness. (Matthew 6:22–24 ERV)

Most people will use some sort of hand gestures when they talk. Gestures are very communicative so pay attention so as not to unconsciously communicate negatively in an unintended way. Hands flailing around may communicate anger, frustration, or chaos and add more tension to the situation.

The Countenance

Why art thou cast down, O my soul? and why art thou disquieted within me? hope in God: for I shall yet praise him, who is the health of my countenance, and my God. (Psalm 43:5 KJV)

A songwriter once wrote, "Ain't it funny how what you feel shows on your face." That statement may bear some truth, but through the power of the Holy Ghost working in you, you are able to control your facial expressions, tone of voice, and attitude. While the eyes and face are communicating, so are the hands, arms, and the rest of the body. For example, hands placed on the hips have a certain degree of sassiness that may not come across positively, or hands flailing about may have a negative effect. Even the folding of the arms is generally taken as negative or uninviting posture. Watch out for that stance as well. The positioning of the feet is also a crucial part of nonverbal communication.

Keep It Moving

After you have effectively communicated with your spouse, let it go. It shouldn't have to ruin your entire day. If you allow it to ruin your day, your spouse will be more focused on your attitude than what you have communicated. So let it go; go back to what you were doing. Do not stew over it, but get your mind on something else. If you already had plans to go out and spend time with your spouse, do it anyway. Be mature about it and don't use your attitude and unresponsiveness to make your spouse suffer. It may work for a while, but eventually he won't respond to it. You don't have to be angry or upset for hours or days.

> Be ye angry, and sin not: let not the sun
> go down upon your wrath. (Ephesians
> 4:26 KJV)

You can speak candidly and honestly while maintaining a Christlike attitude, with a soft voice and a beautiful countenance, and still mean what you say and say what you mean. When you behave this way, you eliminate drama and anything that would take the focus off what you communicated. You will be taken seriously and will be highly respected as a woman of character and strength.

Master of Communication

As you master the art of communication, you will begin to see a change in the way your spouse responds to you. Because you choose to grow in your obedience to God, you will desire a thing and not even have to ask for it because your spouse will be so willing to please you because you are pleasing to God.

As you begin to notice these changes taking place in your spouse's behavior, be sure to acknowledge him with praise. Because he is created in the image of God, he loves praise because God loves praise. The more you praise him, the better he will be. Tell him how much you appreciate the two of you talking and having an intelligent conversation together, even if he has not decided to lean in your direction. Or tell him that you appreciate him hearing you out and trying to understand your feelings.

Looking Good

Your physical appearance will play a significant role in setting the stage for approaching your king. When you're ready for a heart-to-heart with your spouse, you want to be at your best as well as looking your best. Remember that when you first met, there was something about you that physically attracted your husband to you. There was some physical quality that appealed to him to the point that he had to get to know you. It still appeals to him. So play up your features and put on makeup if you wear it, but, nevertheless, look nice. You may be thinking that would be a deceitful thing to do, but no, it is a wise thing to do. No one is really that receptive of someone in disarray of character or appearance who is trying to gain and hold attention. But someone with a pleasant voice, with a beautiful countenance and poised appearance, will capture her audience every time.

Esther's Way

One of my favorite books in the bible is Esther. This is a woman to emulate so far as what it takes to approach your king. But first let's look at the first queen. Queen Vashti was beautiful, and King Xerxes wanted to show her off to all his friends. We might look at the king's behavior as sexist or chauvinistic, but ironically many men are similar today. Scores of men want a woman, car, house, and job that wow the other fellows. Men want to have bragging rights especially around their peers.

> Her husband is known in the gates, when he sitteth among the elders of the land. (Proverbs 31:23 KJV)

Crooked Crown

But Queen Vashti refused to come when the king summoned her. Her behavior was looked upon as disrespectful. Ladies, the worst possible thing we can do as wives is to disrespect our husbands anytime but especially in front of others. To embarrass your husband in front of others will do irreparable damage. If you are fortunate enough to repair the damage, it will take plenty of work and a dreadfully long time before he will trust you again.

The king's advisers felt that once word got out about Vashti's behavior; then none of the men in the kingdom would get any respect from their wives.

In my role as copastor alongside my husband, I can relate very well to this. I remember once we were in church and my husband called me to the front of the church to whisper something to me, and it was obvious that it wasn't what I wanted to hear, but when I turned around, every eye in the church was on me to see what my response would be. I learned that day how much power I had in the ministry. I realized that I held power to make or break the ministry by my behavior especially in the presence of others. I chose to present myself in a way that other women could emulate and be a blessing to my husband and to ministry. Whatever the issue was, it could be dealt with later.

So Vashti was banished from the presence of the king. And a search was started for a new queen.

Outstanding Queen

Esther stood out among all the virgins and gained the king's favor. How? First, she had an ear to hear. She was able to accept instruction. She inquired of the eunuch and was willing to do exactly as instructed, and so she became queen.

Later, when Esther learned of a plot against the king, she informed the king, which proved that she was looking out for his welfare and that she had his back. When your man knows that you have his back, you gain much favor in his eyes.

In chapter 5, it is evident to Esther that she must approach the king on this very important matter of saving the lives of her people; a matter to which a decision had already been sanctioned by the king. Esther knew the possible outcome, so she went into preparation mode. She didn't go bursting in frantically with her hair standing on her head. Esther remained composed although she was distressed. It's hard to think straight when emotions are high, and the mind is discombobulated.

This mentality will cause one to make rash and hasty decisions that are usually bad decisions. But Esther remained calm and went to God in prayer and fasting before she attempted to address her husband, the king. She understood the God-ordained authority and position of power that her husband held.

Keep It Orderly

> But I want you to understand that Christ
> is the Head of every man, and the man is
> the head of a woman, and God is the Head
> of Christ. (1 Corinthians 11:3 NASB)

It is wise to accept God's design and order. When God
gives you a king in your life, He will use that king to
be a blessing and a source of protection and covering for
you. The thing that Esther needed, God would allow it to
come from the hand and heart of her husband. Therefore,
she knew that the best way to approach her husband was
to go through God because God is the ultimate authority.
Many issues would be easily resolved if we were to seek
God first before taking matters into our own hands.

> Trust in the LORD with all thine
> heart; and lean not unto thine own
> understanding. In all thy ways
> acknowledge him, and he shall direct
> thy paths. (Proverbs 3:5–6 KJV)

Getting What You Want

So Esther dressed up in her royal robes, her queenly attire, and approached the king in such a way that he was pleased to see her. More than likely, her beauty had played an important part of King Xerxes's attraction to her, and there is nothing wrong with a little reminder of that attraction. Especially when you are about to consult with your king about an important issue, making yourself attractive will yield far better results than that old comfy house robe and scruffy hair. There is wisdom in using all your assets when approaching your king.

King Xerxes saw Esther standing in the court looking beautiful, and he extended his scepter. She understood that either she would be received or rejected by her husband and had only one opportunity to get it right. She had obtained favor in his sight. Once favor has been obtained with your king, there won't be much that he is not willing to do for you; therefore, once you have obtained his favor, don't abuse it with childish whims.

A Strong Queen

Esther exhibited a quiet strength even though the matter was crucial. No tears, no drama, no panic but composed strength as she drew closer to her king. We should know our king well enough to know the best method of approach to get results. Sometimes, as women, our emotions can overtake us. We may feel that we are "keeping it 100 or being real" because we express anxiety, anger, frustrations, with body language to prove it, but after a while this way will most likely prove to be ineffective, and we wonder why our king will not listen or receive us.

Esther's way, the stage was set. The king was ready to hear whatever Esther had to say.

King Xerxes asked Esther what her desire was and said that he was willing to grant it, even up to half of the kingdom. How's that for an attention grabber?

A Wise Queen

But having his attention was not enough. The wise queen understood the timing principle, and this was not the best time to make her petition known. Good timing is key.

Now even though Esther had not made a petition, the king knew that she wanted something, and he was anxious to do it. But Esther is still setting the stage for the precise time she should be straightforward with the king. Consider that this is about as serious a matter as could be, yet she waits for the right time. Just check out this humble approach by Queen Esther. First, she wants to know if the king is pleased with her—if she has found favor with him before she makes her request. It is wise to be on your husband's good side before you make your petition known.

The virtuous woman in Proverbs 31 exemplifies personal character traits of strength and wisdom that even cause her husband to be praised among his peers.

> Her husband is respected at the city gate,
> where he takes his seat among the elders
> of the land. (Proverbs 31:23 NIV)

Pleasing Your King

Your king is pleased when he is respected by you, especially when others are present. Remember that King Xerxes divorced the first queen, Vashti, because she embarrassed him in front of his guests and made him look bad. No man wants to be embarrassed by anyone but especially not by his wife. When it's obvious that he is respected, then that respect is recognized by his peers. The worst possible thing a queen could ever do is to make her king look bad or weak around others. If people see the queen as bossy and wearing the pants in the relationship, though it might not ever be verbalized by your king, his peers, or even your peers, trust that it is known, and it speaks volumes.

> I beseech you therefore, brethren, by the mercies of God, that you present your bodies a living sacrifice, holy, acceptable to God, which is your reasonable service. (Romans 12:1 NKJV)

The Presentation

The word of God lets us know that there is a way of presenting ourselves that is pleasing and acceptable to Him. The same principle is true with your king. Esther first wanted to make sure that her God was pleased and then her king.

As Esther begins her request, she starts by conveying how she feels. She doesn't start off passing the blame onto Haman. She didn't take the opportunity to diminish his role by telling him that he wasn't a good king or that he had made a bad or uninformed decision. She didn't start the conversation with any "you" statements but merely shared her concerns with the king. She doesn't give more information than is needed. Text or content of your message is essential.

> Let your speech be always with grace, seasoned with salt, that ye may know how ye ought to answer every man. (Colossians 4:6 KJV)

Choosing Your Battles

The king has to ask Esther to name the person who is troubling her. She also informs the king that if this were not extremely important, she would not have bothered him with it. Ladies, some things are too trivial to mention. Don't sweat the small stuff, but choose your battles. Some things are more trouble than they're worth and you don't want to come off as nitpicking or faultfinding.

> It is better to dwell in a corner of the housetop [on the flat roof, exposed to the weather] Than in a house shared with a quarrelsome, (contentious) woman. (Proverbs 21:9 AB)

Submissive Authority

Even after the king had spared Esther and her uncle Mordecai's life and put them in charge of Haman's estate, the totality of Esther's request had not been fully granted. Esther was concerned with more than herself and her immediate family; she was concerned with her overall family, and the stay for the execution of her people had not yet been arranged. Again she petitioned the king in the most sincere of postures and asked for the lives of her people to be spared.

When our spouses understand the true nature of our hearts, which is our concern for the benefit of all, our king will be apt to grant us our request. Not only does the king grant Esther's request, but he trusts her good judgment enough that he tells her to write whatever decree she decides on as it relates to the people. As I mentioned, I copastor alongside my husband in ministry, and although I know he trusts my judgment, I don't run ahead of him making decisions of which he is uninformed. Usually once he has been informed by me of my intentions; I usually get the go-ahead. He trusts that I have given careful consideration to details and that I am acting in accord with and for the well-being of everyone involved. When your spouse knows that he is respected by you and understands that you regard him as your head; then and only then will he be able to relax and gain confidence in you.

Victorious Queen

For the husband is head of the wife as Christ is the Head of the church, Himself the Savior of [His] body. (Ephesians 5:23 AMP)

Ladies, please do not exhaust yourselves by wrestling with God's order. You are not big enough, bad enough, or strong enough to win against Almighty God. You can't win a wrestling match with God or even your spouse, and it's just too frustrating to try. But the good news is that God made provision for us when we follow His guidance. The Bible is filled with women who obeyed the word of God and got the desired response from their men. God will move on your behalf if you are obedient to Him. He will touch your husband's heart. Your king, as tough as he may be, he is not too hard for God.

A Patient Queen

> The king's heart is in the hand of the
> LORD, as the rivers of water: he turneth
> it whithersoever he will. (Proverbs
> 21:1 KJV)

During your prayer and devotion, seek God for wisdom
and insight on how to gain or recapture the favor of
your husband. Ask God to use you as his vessel of
honor in ministering to your husband. Allow God to
strengthen you as you walk faithfully in your powerful
role as a woman and help you to patiently wait for God
to turn the king's heart in your direction.

A Queen's Testimony

I remember when I first gave my life to Christ. I was saved about a year before my husband, and it seemed as if his behavior became increasingly worse. I was doing everything in my power to live a life of holiness. I wanted my husband to be saved and attend church with me. So I browbeat him every Sunday and told him what he should do and how he should do it. And he continued to retreat further and further away from me. I went in prayer, and I told God all about it. I said, "God, I want you to fix my husband; he is all messed up, just a rank sinner. Of course, I expected God to be on my side; after all, I was saved and sanctified. But the Holy Spirit spoke to me and said, "You have given your life to me, so you are the one that I will change and deal with and that will change everything. I was thrown aback. I felt that he (my husband) needed fixing much more than I did. Some of you may feel that way too. I encourage you to let God teach you how to be a godly wife, a virtuous woman; it will make all the difference in the world.

A Queen's Approach

So I changed the way I approached my husband. I began to ask him rather than tell him. I used suggestions. For example, I would say, "I would really love for you to go to church with me," and if he said no, I would kiss him and head out for church. I would return home full of genuine joy, excitement, and positive things to say about the ministry. I wasn't really aware of it, but he was watching me like a hawk, and I was letting my light shine. Once I prepared a candlelight dinner for us. I set the table with red roses and filled the atmosphere with soft music. When he came home and saw what I had done, he seemed almost nervous as he sat down. It had been a bad week for him, and he knew that he hadn't done anything deserving of such treatment. My goal was to win my husband for Christ, and I had a whatever-it-takes attitude. Another time, I bought him a really beautiful outfit. I laid it out on the bed and waited for him to come home. He made it home, but the paycheck did not. He looked sad as I explained that I would have to take it back because we couldn't afford to keep it.

> We prove ourselves by our purity, our understanding, our patience, our kindness, by the Holy Spirit within us, and by our sincere love. (2 Corinthians 6:6 NLT)

One day after about a year, he said, "I think I'll go to church with you this Sunday," and from that day forward our relationship began to mend and take on a new direction. He finally confessed to me one day that all these things were very impactful and played a major role in his life. Now whenever he talks about that time in our lives, he never fails to mention those acts of kindness shown to him by his queen especially at a time when he didn't feel that he deserved it. That had a much more positive effect on him than my previous behavior. God's way yields God's results.

A Queen's Influence

Esther was always the person to seek godly counsel and advice. She sought counsel from her wise cousin and guardian, Mordecai, and from the eunuch, and was led by the Spirit of God, which caused her to make wise decisions.

She made God-inspired decisions and used good judgment as well as her influence regarding her husband in such a way that it was a victory for everyone—herself, her king, and her people, God's people. I imagine that if she hadn't the wisdom to know when and how to approach her husband, he could have been in serious trouble with God. When we use our influence in a way that is Spirit led, we are truly a blessing and a good helpmeet to our husbands. Some women will use their influence for their own benefit and selfish desires. It's possible to use our influence for personal gain like getting him to do the honey-do list or meeting some requirement that we feel is important. Some women have no problem speaking up for things concerning themselves but will quietly stand by and watch their husbands operate outside of the will of God and not say a word to him. Then in a false sense of spirituality say, "I'm praying about it; I'm believing God to touch his heart." While praying is definitely in order, there are times when action is required. The position of helpmeet is an extremely important one. We have a responsibility to convey to our husbands in the most humble way that God knew that he would need our help even if he doesn't. We are to help our husbands reach their spiritual destiny, but we must be very skillful in doing so.

> And the LORD God said, [It is] not good that the man should be alone; I will make him an help meet for him. (Genesis 2:18 KJV)

That's why it is so important to establish a relationship of trust and confidence so that our husbands will seek and value our opinions and advice.

Timing, text, tone, and temperament will be imperative in fulfilling our role as godly wives.

Queen's Timing

Timing according to the dictionary means the choice, judgment, or control of when something should be done.

It is so critical to know when to address a matter. You've heard it said that "Timing is everything." The right thing done at the wrong time can be disastrous. The moment that something happens is usually not the time to discuss it for several reasons. As we mentioned earlier, a deliberating process needs to take place. One has to get in touch with feelings and emotions, not to operate in them but to adequately express them. If others are present, it's probably not good timing. You might say, "Well if I am offended by some remark or behavior, I'm going to address it right then and there. Many an argument has ensued because of bad timing, and generally the desired outcome won't be reached. There have been times when I have waited days, weeks, even months for the right time to bring up a particular subject, in the meantime sorting through my own thoughts and emotions.

Even rehearsing in my mind how it would all play out and if I would get the desired results. After all, good positive results are the goal. Now if I want to inflict pain and discomfort on him, oh yes, I know exactly how to do that. But what would it profit me? Would God be pleased? I found out that if I asked God to, He would give me what I call a divine appointment, a perfect opportunity to discuss the matter in a calm and persuasive way that would touch my king's heart because after all, he knows that it is his job to cover and protect me from hurt, harm and danger. On occasion he has opened the discussion on his own and apologetically expressed genuine sorrow for making me feel discomfort, and all I had to do was humbly accept. Yes, an unwise person might respond in a more aggressive or unappreciative way but probably wouldn't get many more opportunities to do so. Therefore the choices we make, the judgments we use, as well as the control or restraint that we exercise in the heat of the moment, determines the outcome, good or bad.

Queen's Text

My own definition for text is a body of words that compile a message that is conveyed to a listener so that the person might be able to decode and gain knowledge and understanding for discussion and/or examination.

When expressing our truest feelings, it is so important to present the text in its simplicity. This is not the time to embellish (by adding extra details and stretching the truth with phrases like, "you never or you always") or to add unnecessary words.

> Let your speech be always with grace,
> seasoned with salt, that ye may know
> how ye ought to answer every man.
> (Colossians 4:6 KJV)

Grace is a godly attribute. God gives us grace not because we deserve it but because He is full of love and mercy. When we speak to our spouses, God expects us to exhibit that same grace in our speech. I cannot imagine that there would be any trace of hostility, bitterness, or hatefulness but truthfulness wrapped up in love and compassion whether we feel it is deserved.

We never want to come off as nagging, complaining, or faultfinding. Who knows better than a wife how to get the right response out of her husband? Esther, after prayer and most likely the study of her king, knew the possibilities of what could happen and therefore understood the best way to approach him. After all, her life depended on it. The word of God tells us that we ought to know how to answer. I often say that I have a degree in McArlogy (McArthur, my husband).

I should know the words that will get a rise out of him or the words that will calm him down. My purpose in speaking is so that he might gain better knowledge of my perspective and to create an atmosphere conducive for discussion. Sometimes the timing is not right for discussion, and this is an important factor because he will need to decode the message and examine its motives and intentions. This takes time. Meanwhile patience is a virtue. Some women oftentimes will want an immediate response.

Hopefully now that you see the benefit of timing and deliberation, you will offer your spouse the same courtesy.

Queen's Tone

I've often heard it said that a woman sets the tone in her household. She has the power to set the atmosphere in her environment. If she is a lover of peace, she will be an example of peace, and if she loves order, she will be intentional about creating that mood and bringing that positive energy.

We also can think of tone as it regards vocal sounds. When listening to a singer, we listen for the beautiful tones in the voice, but if we don't hear them, we have a tendency to tune them out. The same is true when listening to someone who is speaking, if the tone is too irritating or too harsh. A tone that is too loud is a not so subtle signal that emotions, tensions, and intentions are also escalated.

While it is true that we all have our own way of expressing ourselves, that doesn't excuse the fact that we must be willing to work on and cultivate our delivery.

Some people's tone can go from 1 to 10 when speaking.

The more excited, the more urgency or even irritation will be apparent in the inflection of words. And that can possibly change the whole message and deflect from the listener's receptivity.

Tone conveys so much additional information to a message. Tone will express if a person is feeling tense. Tone sends a message of the mood of the speaker. The polarity determines if the message is coming across as negative or positive.

Certain tones can make our message come across as pleasant and polite or irrational and pushy. The goal here is to determine how you want to be perceived and what is the desired outcome.

If a positive result is desired, one that will benefit everyone, then a calm tone is the way to go. Be clear and state the facts in a peaceful, nonthreatening tone.

A monotone voice, while it may be lower in volume, can have a placating vibe that still will not come across as authentic. This tone will not be convincing of a genuine desire to have honest and effective communication but rather is a mockery and lacks real value. Here is a list of tone detectors that will help you to identify and evaluate your tone because it communicates so much more than your words and will be a determining factor in your spouse's response.

Be honest with yourself. What emotions and moods do your tones reflect?

Are you getting the desired response from your spouse?

Ask your listener how you come across and let it be known that you are working on it.

Refine your tone strategy and use words, gestures, and tone that fit the message.

List of detailed tone descriptors:

authoritative
caring
cheerful
coarse
conservative
conversational
casual
dry
edgy
enthusiastic
formal
frank
friendly
fun
funny
humorous
informative
irreverent

matter-of-fact
nostalgic
passionate
playful
professional
provocative
quirky
respectful
romantic
sarcastic
serious
smart
sympathetic
trustworthy
unapologetic
upbeat
witty

Soft Happiness	Mood State Happiness	Intense Happiness
Smiling	Happy	Elated
Upbeat	Glad	Exhilarated
Peaceful	Content	Manic
Calm	Optimistic	Giddy
Amused	Cheerful	Euphoric
Open	Joyful	Awe-filled
Friendly	Satisfied	Blissful
Encouraged	Lively	Enthralled
Hopeful	Delighted	Rapturous
Inspired	Pleased	Jubilant
Jovial	Gratified	Ecstatic
	Excited	Overjoyed
	Gleeful	Radiant
	Merry	
	Playful	

Soft Anger	Mood State Anger	Intense Anger
Annoyed	Angry	Hostile
Frustrated	Mad	Aggressive
Cross	Offended	Livid
Apathetic	Antagonized	Outraged
Peeved	Bristling	Furious
Irritated	Sarcastic	Belligerent
Cranky	Aggravated	Hateful
Crabby	Arrogant	Bitter
Bored	Indignant	Raving
Impatient	Inflamed	Contemptuous
Critical	Affronted	Disgusted
Cold	Resentful	Vengeful
Displeased	Incensed	Vindictive
Rankled	Exasperated	Violent
Detached	Riled up	Menacing
Indifferent		Seething
		Spiteful

Soft Fear	Mood State Fear	Intense Fear
Alert	Fearful	Terrorized
Hesitant	Afraid	Shocked
Pensive	Suspicious	Panicked
Watchful	Startled	Filled with Dread
Cautious	Unnerved	Horrified
Curious	Anxious	Phobic
Leery	Nervous	Petrified
Uneasy	Worried	Paralyzed
Doubtful	Alarmed	
Confused	Shaky	
Fidgety	Perturbed	
Apprehensive	Aversive	
Shy	Wary	
Concerned	Distrustful	
Disquieted	Rattled	
Timid	Unsettled	
Edgy	Jumpy	
Disconcerted		
Insecure		
Indecisive		
Disoriented		

And be not conformed to this world:
but be ye transformed by the renewing
of your mind, that ye may prove what is
that good, and acceptable, and perfect,
will of God. (Romans 12:2 KJV)

Queen's Temperament

Temperament is our unique personality trait. It's the way we think and act. It's also the way we interact in the world in which we live as well how we react to those around us.

Temperament plays a big part in a person's mood, whether one comes across as negative or positive, introverts or extroverts. Some temperaments may have an outgoing, fun-loving, laid-back kind of attitude. Another may be a more serious and worrying type. One may be impulsive and easily excited. Yet another may be cool, calm, and collected. The good news here is that our Creator, who knows all about us and our individual personalities, calls us to be transformed by the renewing of our minds and be conformed to the image of Jesus Christ, which enables us to do God's perfect will regardless of our personalities.

I remind myself daily to forget everything you thought you knew before you accepted Jesus as your Savior and Lord; it was all wrong.

> Let this mind be in you, which was also
> in Christ Jesus. (Philippians 2:5 KJV)

Scripture tells us to let this mind be in you—the mind of Jesus Christ.

God can get the glory out of our lives regardless of our unique personalities because His strength is made perfect in our weaknesses.

> But he said to me, "My grace is sufficient
> for you, for my power is made perfect
> in weakness." Therefore I will boast all
> the more gladly about my weaknesses,
> so that Christ's power may rest on me.
> (2 Corinthians 12:9 KJV)

So, therefore, any weaknesses in our temperament do not have to hinder us getting the results we want. Allow the Holy Spirit to be in control of your temperament especially when trying to communicate and relate information to your king.

Ultimately, the queen's temperament is one that is completely surrendered and totally yielded to Jesus Christ.

Remember, queen's rule is exemplifying a particular standard of God's goodness and righteousness in our conduct in how to engage with our kings. When we do it God's way, we get God's results and always win in *The End.*

> Let all things be done decently and in
> order. (1 Corinthians 14:40)

Printed in the United States
by Baker & Taylor Publisher Services